Friday

by Mary Lindeen • illustrated by Javier González

Content Consultant: Susan Kesselring, M.A., Literacy Educator and Preschool Director

magic wagon

NOV   2008

visit us at
www.abdopublishing.com

Published by Magic Wagon, a division of the ABDO Publishing Group, 8000 West 78th Street, Edina, Minnesota, 55439. Copyright © 2008 by Abdo Consulting Group, Inc. International copyrights reserved in all countries. All rights reserved. No part of this book may be reproduced in any form without written permission from the publisher. Looking Glass Library™ is a trademark and logo of Magic Wagon.

Printed in the United States.

Text by Mary Lindeen
Illustrations by Javier González
Edited by Patricia Stockland
Interior layout and design by Becky Daum
Cover design by Becky Daum

Library of Congress Cataloging-in-Publication Data

Lindeen, Mary.
  Friday / Mary Lindeen ; illustrated by Javier A. González ; content consultant, Susan Kesselring.
     p. cm. —— (Days of the week)
  Includes bibliographical references.
  ISBN 978-1-60270-101-4
  I. Days—Juvenile literature. I. González, Javier A., 1974– ill. II. Kesselring, Susan. III. Title.
  GR930.L56 2008
  529'.1—dc22

                                    2007034055

Seven days in a week

are always the same.

What's the day after Thursday?

Do you know its name?

It's Friday! You said it!

There is nothing to fix!

You knew the right answer.

Friday's day number six.

Some silly people

who have not read this book

might think that "Fry" day

is a time when we cook.

While Friday might be
a day to bake sweets,
there's lots you can do
to make Friday neat.

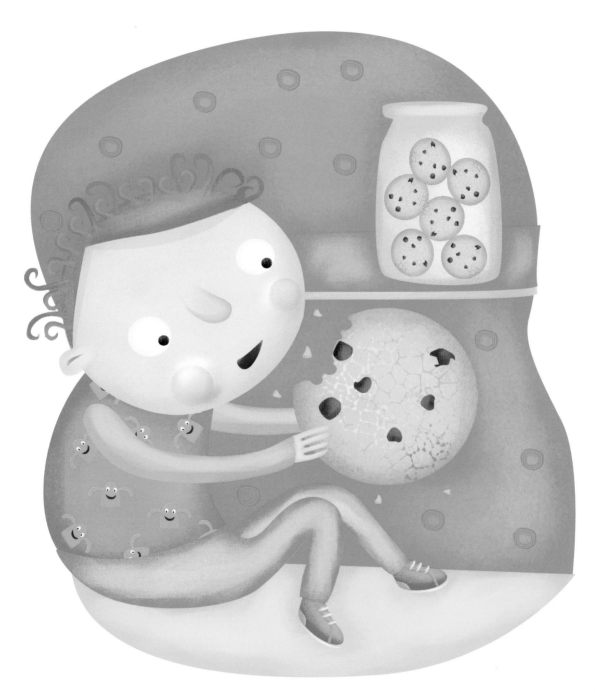

"Thank goodness it's Friday,"
some people say.
They're happy that Saturday's
next on the way.

But Friday is great!
Don't hurry to end it.
Friday's a fun day,
if you know how to spend it.

14

A Friday in April is all about trees.

We think about how they help birds, you, and me.

For some people,
Friday's the night to go out

to supper, a show,
or a ball game to shout.

17

Many people love Fridays for staying up late.

With no school tomorrow,

they can sleep way past eight.

Now Friday is over,

and the weekend is near.

Rest up for tomorrow.

Saturday's almost here!

The Days of the Week

1 Sunday

2 Monday

3 Tuesday

4 Wednesday

7
Saturday

6
Friday

5
Thursday

SEE A FRIDAY PICTURE SHOW

Get your friends and family together. Select a video or DVD that you will all enjoy. Then make some popcorn, turn out the lights, and pretend you are at the movie theater on a Friday night.

TREES ARE TERRIFIC!

Arbor Day is celebrated on the last Friday in April. In honor of Arbor Day, do something nice for a tree near you. Give it some water, clean up the ground beneath its branches, or just give it a big hug!

WORDS TO KNOW

fry: to cook food in hot oil.

morning: the time of day between sunrise and noon.

weekday: any day of the week except Saturday or Sunday.

weekend: the days at the beginning and end of the week; Saturday and Sunday.